# BECAUSE YOU CAN

Loving those who have a hard time loving themselves.

Lessons learned from care giving for those with physical, mental, and emotional illnesses, and broken hearts.

Keitha J. James

Copyright © 2011 by Keitha James
Web Site: BecauseYouCan.kjj2011.weebly.com
All rights reserved
Printed in the United States of America

ISBN 978-1-604-58-833-0
Library of Congress Cataloging in Publication Data


Published by Instant Publisher


Scripture quotations have been taken from the NRIV Bible
Copyright © 1989
By Thomas Nelson Publishers in Nashville, Tennessee


This book is not meant to be therapy or counseling, nor does it provide clinical advice or treatment. Readers are advised to consult physicians or professional mental or medical health providers when dealing with mental health and medical issues. The author holds no responsibility for any possible consequences from any treatment, action or application of information in this book to any particular reader. Some names have been changed for their privacy.

This book is dedicated to my brother,
Dale,
who teaches me everyday
to live life to the fullest
through the challenges handed you.

# Ecclesiastes 3:1-8  NRS

For everything there is a season, and a time for every matter under heaven:

A time to be born, and a time to die;

A time to plant, and a time to pluck up what is planted;

A time to kill, and a time to heal;

A time to break down, a time to build up;

A time to weep, and a time to laugh;

A time to mourn, and a time to dance;

A time to throw away stones, and a time to gather stones together;

A time to embrace, and a time to refrain from embracing;

A time to seek, and a time to lose;

A time to keep, and a time to throw away;

A time to tear, and a time to sew;

A time to keep silence, and a time to speak

A time to love, and a time to hate;

A time for war, and a time for peace.

# ACKNOWLEDGEMENT

Why write a book when there are millions of books out there to be read on this same subject? Inspiration is what caused me to write and spiritual growth called me to express my life's journey with people and this world in which we travel. I was encouraged to write about the people I work with when I first went into physical therapy by my pastor and friend, Mark Saline. I said I would think about it. I had written in journals most of my life. I like to write but, did not feel I was a "Writer."

As I moved forward through the years, said goodbye to my earthly parents and was blessed with a grandchild in between their passing, I became more reflective on my life and how I viewed living in this time and place. I have been blessed beyond measure with the caring of people. My family has always loved and encouraged me on all my paths. Reverend Mark Saline, Reverend Bill Williamson, Reverend Smith, and Reverend "Mac" McDowell have been great inspirational people in my life. They showed me how each of us can be ministers in our own lives with the confidence that only God can give us. They challenged me as a lay leader to go beyond my expectations of myself and let our Higher Power work through us and bless us. Thank you to all of you people in the ministry that truly walk in God's grace.

To my husband, Michael, who has always encouraged me if not pushed me at times to be my best. I am forever grateful to the soul mate that has traveled with me for over 36 years now. You encouraged me when I needed it, loved me when I was unlovable, and walked the walk with me in your own way. Thank you.

To my daughter, Carissa and granddaughter, Ashlind which are two of the many abundances of God's blessings in my life. I am blessed every day I am with you both. Thank you for your honesty, your laughter, and your ever eternal love. Each generation has much to teach. I am eternally grateful for your presence filling my life with unexpected blessings and lessons every day.

My siblings: Millie, Danny, Lorri, Dale, Maureen, Dara, and our three brothers who we will meet on the other side after we leave this earth. I am forever grateful for the early years of living with a community and its many different types. We learned to socialize before we even stepped out into the world. Much did we learn, having each other's support when we needed it, enjoying time together when we can, good and trying times. Thank you for all the lessons I have learned from you. Even the brothers who passed as babies, many lessons have we learned from beyond. Thank you. My "brother," Jerry who has been in my life longer than some siblings, thank you for your steady presence and love.

To my dear friends Carolyn Acton and Julie Tidwell thank you for assisting me with the initial layout and editing of this book. You will never know how grateful I am for filling in the areas I am so weak at. Thank you and God's Blessings be with you always. Any errors contained in this book are of course mine.

There are too many people that have come and gone in my life to thank that have inspired me. I have said goodbye to many patients, whether they went home or moved on from this world. The lessons you have taught me are simple yet priceless. Thank you.

Last but not least, my friends. From junior high to now, all the friends that have been in my life have inspired me to learn more, pray deeper, and walk the walk together in life with joy and support, laughter and tears.

In January of this year, 2011, I went on a cruise with all motivational speakers. One in particular said something I did not forget. Wayne Dyer stated; "Most of you will come here and listen to how you can advance your life but most of you will go back home and return to the same life you have always known. But a few will be forever changed." I want to be one of the few that grow stronger in spirit and fulfill my purpose. Thank you, Wayne Dyer, for the challenge.

# PREFACE

When you befriend the frail aging, the sick, mentally distressed, and emotionally distraught people in society, be prepared for a journey of joy, of suffering, of sorrow, of wisdom, and great peace. Love them, listen to them, touch them, laugh and cry with them. Wash their feet and tend to their needs. Then you are serving the Divinity of the whole person, unconditionally. Embrace the moment, for it becomes a memory too soon. No barriers, no boundaries, just love for each other.

The joy of being in their presence of having lived life eases our worries of what is to come. The suffering of their losses let us know we are not alone. The wisdom of their knowledge and advice of living far surpasses any book that could educate us on their experience with life. The peace they bring forth in their daily and simplistic living teaches us to embrace this world one moment at a time and enjoy whatever it is we are able to do. I have been blessed to be able to sit at the feet of the aging, the dying, the isolated and lonely people who have given me so much wisdom and peace. Thank you all, I am forever indebted to you.

From my time with these precious folk, I have learned to be more prayerful, listen better, hug more, serve others more sacredly, live simple, spend quiet time with God, enjoy nature, and embrace the simplicity of chores just because I can. I pray that all people have the chance to befriend and care for other human beings at one time in their life whether it is a relative, a friend or even a stranger soon to become a friend. Learn their wisdom from life, experience their grace with the ending phase of their journey on earth, and be filled with their stories so you too can be uplifted as you age or become ill. Draw from their strength and lessons. So these lessons begin.

## CONTENTS

| | | |
|---|---|---|
| 1 | Reasons We Don't Love Ourselves | 1 |
| 2 | Lessons Learned In My Early Years | 3 |
| 3 | Lessons Learned After High School | 10 |
| 4 | Lessons Learned In Mid Years | 16 |
| 5 | Always be Prayerful and Confident | 20 |
| 6 | Lessons Learned In Times Of Change | 30 |
| 7 | Use of Interests and Hobbies to Help Heal | 32 |
| 8 | Be in Their World | 33 |
| 9 | Time Alone | 35 |
| 10 | Special Treatment | 37 |
| 11 | Expect to be Blessed | 39 |
| 12 | Don't Try Be Everything | 41 |
| 13 | Be There for the Lonely and Depressed | 44 |
| 14 | Responsibility | 46 |
| 15 | Continual Care | 48 |
| 16 | Know When Your Caring is Finished | 49 |
| 17 | Teach the Generations | 51 |
| 18 | Practice Tolerance | 54 |
| 19 | Unlimited Potential | 56 |
| 20 | Know Your Gifts / Live Through Your Heart | 58 |
| 21 | Communal Living | 60 |
| 22 | Forgive and Move Forward | 62 |
| 23 | Learn Empathy | 63 |
| 24 | Visiting the Sick | 66 |
| 25 | Be Open Minded | 68 |
| 26 | Keep The Environment Safe and Healthy | 69 |
| 27 | Be Grateful, at Peace, and Full of Joy | 75 |
| | Conclusion | 78 |

## REASONS WE DON'T LOVE OURSELVES

It is difficult to come to the point of no longer loving or being able to care for yourself. Sometimes it is the simple image you have when you look into the mirror, we don't like what we see physically or the person we see mentally. Perhaps it stems from verbal or physical abuse that gives you the feeling of low self-esteem, or even worse, feeling worthless and useless in this world. God doesn't make junk.

Sometimes it is an illness where you cannot help yourself. Sometimes it's a learning disability and feeling stupid. It could be the expectations you place on yourself that are too high or unachievable. It could be hormonal or something not diagnosed yet. Depression leaves you hopeless. Obesity leaves you helpless at times, and can lead to illness. Any disease can make one angry and extremely vulnerable, especially when they are placing the choices of their life into other's hands. Aging causes one to doubt their talents and gifts of wisdom when ill. The body can leave us delusional.

Other reasons for not loving yourself can be that you are a child of divorced parents and feel it may have been your fault such as; being orphaned or a foster child, being a single parent, or being different such as ethnicity, disabled, or speech impediment. Maybe one has a disease that no one wants to care for due to fear of not enough knowledge about the disease. Being poor can be another thing that leaves us hopeless, (not always), wounded emotionally, or bullied. All these and more can leave you devastated, hopeless, and helpless at times. There are many more reasons, these are just some. This is the time when someone needs to be aware of another person's difficult situation and be there for them.

Three ways of being there for someone are: physically, emotionally, and spiritually.

<u>Physically</u> be there for them.  Tend to their physical needs and make it as easy as possible to make their quality of life good.  You can physically be in their presence, and they may only require company and silence.

<u>Emotionally</u> you can empathize with them.  You can share laughter, be their advocate, and express to them you will do what it takes to make them better.

<u>Spiritually</u> you can pray with them or for them.  You can express your strength in God, and read inspirational words to encourage them.

# LESSONS LEARNED IN MY EARLY YEARS

My journey for quality of life in all aspects started in the home I grew up in. I was one of ten children, three of whom I never knew due to being stillborn or living only 12 hours. These are my brothers I know in Spirit. I have been blessed with four sisters and two brothers whom shaped my early years.

One particular sibling, my younger brother Dale, stuttered. We were sixteen months apart and inseparable as my mother would say. Dale was timid and shy, so early on I became his advocate. I interpreted for him, I became his voice. My mother use to say I would get mad when people could not understand what Dale was saying because I knew exactly what he wanted. I also got into many fights as we grew up protecting him from bullies and arrogant egos. When Dale entered kindergarten, the teacher told my mom to make sure we gave Dale time to speak without interruption. So for many months my mom had to stop all conversation when Dale spoke. Eventually Dale stopped stuttering. Trying to get a word in edge wise with a lot of children was pretty difficult. As we grew, Dale told me he could fight his own fights and did so from that point on, but still got me into a few! **My first lesson on this journey of caring was being the voice of someone who couldn't express it himself.**

Our family moved many times during my elementary years, so I didn't make close friends, Dale was my friend. When we finally settled into a home, I was twelve years old and still felt like an outsider trying to fit in. I connected with the underdogs.

I grew up in a neighborhood of boys, and became athletic, competing with boys. This became an advantage for me. I had protected my brother from most of the boys in the early years.

When I went to school, I became friends with everyone, but I connected with the underdogs more. They were quiet people that went to school, did what was required, and went back home. Some were very studious, some were extremely shy, and some didn't feel like they fit anywhere. There were kids intimidated by bullies, and some were outgoing and good at everything, but never belonged to the elite group or clicks. I was blessed with my athletic abilities so I could mingle with the other athletes, but I always felt more connected with those that felt left out or not good enough. These were the achievers! They just didn't know it. **They inspired me to be a better person! They inspired me to be more compassionate, have more empathy.** They are the heroes! I learned to let all people know they are important. God doesn't make junk. He makes beautiful butterflies that sometimes take longer to come out of their cocoon. But beautiful do they become!

If you think back to your younger years, you too will see all the lessons early on that will have led you to the person you are today. You have a choice to move beyond the adversities in life and enjoy all life has to offer. I learned to never underestimate people. They all have gifts to offer.

My mother and grandmother influenced me more when I was young. My mother was pregnant and sickly most of my younger years (until I was about 10 years old or so). She was wheelchair bound for about two years when I was five, and I spent a lot of time with my Grandmother, my mother's mother. Our uncle told us years later that the doctors thought it was a mental issue, but my mom swore she had multiple sclerosis. Mental illness ran on my mother's side of the family. My mother had several mental breakdowns (that is what they called it when I was a child) and would be gone for a month at a time in which the siblings would be split up and given to friends and relatives until mom was back home. My father was a truck driver and was required to be gone a lot. Kids adjust very quickly and are very protective of each other in situations like this.

My mom went on to be an alcoholic and prescription drug abuser. She was diagnosed as bi-polar. When my mother was stable, she was an immaculate housekeeper, good cook, loved playing board games and cards, was president of the ladies bowling association, and found a lot of humor in life. My mom raised seven children with my grandmother close by to assist. I remember my mother's care with Dale and how she had all of our backs if someone spoke badly about us. Mom's firm hand and teaching us to listen to Dale helped him become secure as a person and one who deserved to be heard. **I learned to be patient at a young age and listen carefully.**

Dale also struggled with school. He averaged C's and D's while the rest of us were on honor roll. Only A's and B's were acceptable to my mom. But when she found out how difficult it was for Dale in school, he became the exception to the rule. But the rest would be grounded with anything less than honor roll. **I learned another lesson. There is always an exception to the rule when needed.** Each person is to be looked at individually and adjustments need to be made if necessary.

When I look back at the care that my older sister, Millie, gave us I thank God for her in my life. Millie was a disciplined, loving and organized person. She made us feel safe and secure when our parents were not around, which was often. Millie kept house, fed us, helped us with our homework and gave up a lot of school activities she could have been in to keep the home stable. We could count on her. I am forever grateful for a wonderful sister who gave up much of her life so we could have a feeling of security and safety. **I learned that it is important for someone to give you the feeling of safety and security, whatever age you are. Sacrifices are hard to do.**

My grandmother was my physical, spiritual, and emotional guardian angel. She always told me how precious I was and how much she loved me. My grandmother grew up the oldest of four girls to a strong Irish-Catholic family, with a father who was the Chief of Police in the town where they lived. My grandmother, Mildred, married one of the town's trouble men, Clinton. She soon became pregnant and moved back home to her parents due to domestic violence abuse. My uncle was born. Mildred went back to Clinton and became pregnant again only to leave and go back home due to the same circumstances. My mother, Larraine, was born. My great-grandfather took the children away from my grandmother until she could prove to be a fit parent. Mildred moved out of town and found work where I grew up. She eventually got my mom and uncle back and raised them as a single parent. My grandmother continued to raise the two until they grew up and moved on. My grandmother called our house every day in the morning and evening to make sure everything was ok. I spent a lot of time with my grandmother in the early years, and watched her live alone, and grieve, and enjoy life. I was with her when the love of her life, George, died. He was her second husband and he loved her too. He died suddenly and was without insurance.

My grandmother lost her restaurant that she and George ran. I watched her suffer the loss of a loved one, loss of her income and come to temporarily depend on her children for all needs. We would visit my grandfather's grave every Saturday with a packed lunch, and stay for hours while my grandmother told George everything that was going on in her life. **I learned to honor the dead. I know somehow, somewhere they are still listening and guiding us.**
My grandmother eventually married and was able to live somewhat comfortably until she passed away in 1981. **My grandmother taught me how to survive, to endure, how to grieve, how to move forward, and how to treat each relationship with great love.**

As a single parent, she taught me the struggles of managing a household and trying to be both parents at the same time, along with the stigma that comes with being a single parent. Until my grandmother passed away, she was always there for my mother, whatever condition my mom was in. My mom was devastated when Mildred died. Only then did she realize what a divine support system she had in my grandmother, and how we take things for granted that are so life-giving. My grandmother called me every night and morning until the day she took her last breath. I still, to this day, look at the phone only to thirst for her voice. But I know she is closer to me now than she was in physical form.

My father, Keith, loved each of us in his own way. He lost his mom at five years old and his dad gave the children up to relatives to remarry. My mother and father's relationship was always rocky but he was determined to keep us together.

He was a patient man when it came to us.

When our mother died, we were gathered together for a week (even though we lived all over) to help settle things. Three years later, we gathered again to say goodbye to our father. We talked, honored and mourned our dad and mother and our memories of them. **I learned to honor the father and mother who raised us the best way they knew how to.** No matter what the losses are, they need to be grieved and shared. **Each loss, not only of the death of a loved one, is important to each individual and we need to respect that.**

In high school I had a friend, Michael, who came over to my home quite often to visit. I tried to set him up with a girl he liked but it did not work out. I had a guy I liked and waited around the phone most of my sophomore and junior years of high school for him to call and ask me out. Mike would tease me and tell me I was wasting my time.

I was chubby in junior high and at that time this boy was the only one that paid attention to me as a girl, I was the other guys buddy. When I realized I was wasting my time, Mike asked me out and we went from there. Mike was the oldest of four children with a sick mom, and a dad who worked a lot to support the family. His father made him responsible for the care of his siblings at a young elementary age. Mike took full responsibility with a positive attitude, and his siblings looked up to him. Expectations were placed on him at a young age. He enjoyed taking care of them, even though he could have felt trapped and cheated from not having a fun filled childhood.

When we were in high school, we worked on a report together. Mike never cared for school much, but took interest when he and I started studying together. We turned in our papers and I received an A. Mike got a low grade and was accused of cheating by copying off me. He put as much work into the paper as I did. He held his head high and said he was use to this treatment. He was full of grace and blew it off. He inspired me while I tried to convince the teachers he did just as much work toward the report as I did. Unfortunately, I did not get any results from it.

When Michael and I married I knew I had made a good choice because of his values in taking care of his siblings, making good choices and determination to get ahead in life. He had a positive attitude, not letting people or events get him down. **I learned to be full of grace with events and people who could have disappointed me, and to be inspired by other's responses toward life's experiences.**

# LESSONS AFTER HIGH SCHOOL

When I graduated from high school, I felt lost in a world I could not fit in, although I did well in school. School was my safe haven and now I had to move on. I grieved for months. No money for college, no car for transportation, and feeling sorry for myself; my mom got fed up and called the school and talked to the co-op teacher who set kids up for part-time work. I looked but could find nothing.

I started my first job as a bagger in a major grocery chain. I worked five months there and went on to work for Montgomery Ward. I knew I got the interview due to my unusual name, because when I went in for the interview, the woman looked at me and looked at my name again. This company was in a predominately black community. I came from a predominately white community. I had no feelings either way of prejudices because I was never exposed to it, probably because I came from a poor community with no status to speak of. **I learned a lesson that day. Sometimes it is not always your experience, but unusual things, such as my name, that gets you in the door of opportunity. The other lesson I learned is, someone is always looking out for you and pushing you forward whether you like it or not.**

Mike and I married in 1975 and had our child, Carissa in 1979. The early years of marriage can be very trying to get to know each other as husband and wife. Each must learn how to live with a new person all over again, to compromise, and love without conditions. I learned a lot about tolerance which I will talk about later.

When our child, Carissa, started school, everything appeared fine. As the end of first grade approached, her grades started to decline. In second grade we continued to work on reading, flash cards, and any resources we could find to stay current with what she was learning.

This did not help, and her grades continually dropped. At a teacher conference we were told she was lazy, a day dreamer and needed to pay attention more. She and I became frustrated and became nervous when we worked together with her homework.

When Carissa was held back in third grade, I ask that she be tested for any problems with learning. She was put on a one year waiting list. So we took her to be tested. She was diagnosed with Dyslexia. I knew my daughter was not lazy, and did pay attention, but I could not figure it out until then. She had a mild form, which they said is harder to detect. Carissa had tutors for the next five years of her life. When she got out of school for the day, she went to a tutor that specialized with this condition, to learn how to comprehend the way she needed to learn. That also built her confidence level up so she felt she was smart, and not the lazy title she was given by some of her teachers.

Carissa was blessed with many good teachers. I fought all through school so she could be the best she was capable of being. **I learned the lesson that you may have to be someone's advocate until they can stand on their own. I have carried this lesson out with all my patients – never, say never!** Carissa went on to finish high school and complete college. **Be someone's cheerleader when they need you.**

When our family moved to Tennessee, I realized I could do anything I wanted to. I could change careers, volunteer, or explore my gifts given to me by God. I decided, after volunteering many places and learning more about myself, that I wanted to go to college and get an education in the field of physical therapy. In the early years of my vocation, students are taught to not get emotionally involved with the patient and keep focused on the goals to be achieved in a limited amount of time. It is a physical problem, deal with the physical issue and move on.

It is pretty simple with orthopedic patients. They are on a higher level most of the time with only one problem to deal with, the body part. Protocol is relatively simple. Fix it, strengthen it back to its best potential, and move on. But, if ones pain is too difficult to manage, then you need to first manage the pain before you can go forward with the healing process. This becomes the emotional part. Now you no longer have to just deal with the physical, but the emotional also. Sometimes it is simple pain management. Sometimes it goes deeper into fear of pain itself. Then we have to go outside the box to problem solve. It becomes a mind game sometimes involving visual imagery to relax, always deep breathing exercises, and max encouragement that this soon will pass. You need to push them where they do not think they can go with an even tone, gentle approach and the confidence that are made of heroes.

After I graduated from college, I decided to go back and spend a month with my family because I knew once I started working I would be limited as to when I could come back. I also did not know this would be the last time I would spend any amount of time with my parents before they passed. My mother was supposed to be using a walker for safety, and was on oxygen all the time.

We went to my parents' vacation spot for ten days. It was about ten minutes from their home. I was observant of mom and her abilities, which were becoming more limited. I helped mom if she asked for it, but let her do as much as she could. We went to the store and mom wanted to go into the store without her oxygen. She was tired of hauling it around, she stated. I said this was not a good idea, but she insisted. So we went as far as the entrance to the door, and she became short winded. I had her sit down and brought back her oxygen (O2). She became very anxious and began to panic, which I knew would cause her to breathe even harder. I told her to look at me and focus. I repeated this several times. Then I told her to follow me and breathe deeply. After a few minutes, she calmed down and was back to breathing her normal pattern. She said thank you for letting her make the decision to try to not use the oxygen because it let her know and decide on her own that she could not be without it. **I learned that day that one needs to decide when they cannot do things anymore, and not have everyone else tell them even if they know.**

Another time after we came home, my mother felt she could still drive and no one would let her. I told her to get in the driver's seat, hooked up her oxygen and said a prayer for God to watch over us and the people we come across. Mom drove out of the driveway and maybe about 300-400 feet down the road and pulled off the road. She said that was all she could do, and realized she was no longer capable of driving but thanked me for letting her come to that decision. Then she asked for me to pray that the Lord would take her, and she would not become a burden to those who love her. I was saddened by my mom's request, but I did pray for her and asked the Lord that she would not suffer. Eleven months later, my mom passed away quietly in her chair. I thanked God for the foresight that allowed me a month, the year prior, to spend with them, only to have dad pass three years later of cancer.

I have experienced both lingering death from cancer and sudden death from cardiac arrest. Neither is easy and goodbyes come too quickly, but the grace of God's peace is always with us. I will always remember the last hug I received from my mother, because she would not let me go and stated she did not want me to go. We both cried, and Dad and Mike pried her hands off me and we left to go back home. I will feel that hug for the rest of my living days here. **Listen to people's unconscious messages. They may be a foretelling of what is to come.** It may also be conscious.

I had a patient right after visiting mom who had cancer. She was 89 years old and was not expected to live long. Ann told me in January that she was going to live until she reached 90, which was September, and then going to be with the Lord. I worked with Ann for a few months until she was strong enough to assist with her care. Ann's birthday came in September. She was still in the center. Her family celebrated her birthday and two days later Ann passed. When I went to her room the day before, as I usually did to say hello, she appeared to be unconscious. The family was talking about her funeral and what was going to whom. They told me she was in a coma and could not hear. I walked over to Alice and told her good morning. I told her to squeeze my hand if she understood me. I received a big squeeze and her family was aghast. I told her I loved her. **I was reminded again, although I had forgotten, that people still hear what is going on and Ann proved that to me that day. I know her family will always remember that too.**

The first time that happened, my mother had surgery for an aneurysm and was in a coma. The CCU nurse kept coming and asking my mother if she was awake, or could she hear him. He stated he was trying to alert the brain to wake up. He repeated this all during his shift with no response. When my mother finally came to, she stated all she could hear was her nurse asking her if she was there. She wanted to say, "Where do you think I am, and please stop asking me those questions. Just let me sleep." Although we saw no body response to the nurse's questions, obviously mom heard them every time but could not physically respond.

# LESSONS LEARNED IN MY MID YEARS

Since our family's longevity is about 70 years old, nursing home/rehabilitation centers were not something I was familiar with. During clinicals, I was in out-patient centers, hospitals, and rehabilitation centers/ long term care facilities. I was not sure I could do this. It included some orthopedic patients, stroke patients, Parkinson patients, a lot of neurological patients, wound care patients, balance disorder patients, dementia/ Alzheimer patients, infectious patients including those in isolation, and patients on ventilators. It was well diversified with the aging population. I would walk in the facility and smell urine or feces, see infections and wounds that would turn my stomach from the looks and smell, colostomy bags that would break, tracheotomies that needed cleaning, and lots of pain. There was dying all around me in the long term section. I was overwhelmed, and thought I would have to go elsewhere. **That is when God stepped in and had me listen clearly to him. He told me this was where I was to serve Him best and would teach me most of life's lessons, as well as master the ones I already know.** Not only did I stay working in these centers, they became life-giving centers for me, many lessons did I learn.

At first I became frustrated because patient's medicines were not given when I thought they should be given. People were in urinated beds and I thought were not changed soon enough. People were not getting the help they needed to eat and patients were not dressed and ready for therapy when I thought they should be. **Listen to what I said. These situations were not appropriate to what I felt they should be. A little arrogant wouldn't you say?** I became more frustrated until I realized I was the problem. I complained to nurses about timely medicine, and to the certified nursing assistant about patient's not being properly cared for with feeding, bathing, and bed changes. I was not the patient's advocate I was the centers nightmare therapist! I was making enemies real quick. When I realized what I was doing, I felt ashamed at my actions and attitude. Good thing this lasted but a short period of time. I remember a Sunday school lesson where we spoke of sympathy verses empathy. I felt bad because I felt my patients were not getting proper care but I did not have the empathy to be the change needed. I prayed God would teach me to empathize with all caregivers, and to bring the best care to our patients working side by side in harmony and in the best interest of all patients.

Always know what you pray for comes forth in abundance. I started by going to each patient's room when I arrived at work to say hello and see if the nurse's assistant needed any help changing the bed, getting patient's to the bathroom or helping them set the patient up for breakfast. I also thanked everyone for helping me with anything I needed, and learning the nurses' routine with medicines. I soon learned how overwhelmed the medical staff was with trying to keep things running in a smooth fashion, without someone demanding attention the way I did. I continued to see to patients needs outside my required box, to assist and help with making a better work environment, and to see patient's in a smooth and timely manner. I worked with short staff nurses to learn how to flush a peg tube so I would not have to call them all the time. I assisted with emptying catheter collection bags, and I helped changed colostomy bags so we could have the patient clean at all times. I worked on the wound team, which included every department of the facility having one representative to see the wound patients and cover the importance of each one's role including housekeeping, dietary, therapy, nursing, and anyone else that was involved in the healing process with the patient. I learned how to clean a tracheostomy, so I would not have to call nursing into isolation rooms to see my patient. I learned to be everyone's advocate. **The lesson I learned was to be a help to everyone. We are all in this together and no one is more important than the other.**

Next, I looked at the patient's routine. Was he or she a morning person or afternoon person? What did they like to eat? What time did they eat at home? How much did they eat usually? If they were an a.m. person, what time did they get up? Did they go to the bathroom when they first got up or wait a little bit? How often did they have bowel movements? When do they bathe? Do they take a shower or bath? What were their hobbies? What did they like to do? Do they socialize or do they like to spend time alone? All these questions are important to the healing of the person while they are in the centers recuperating. The better you can keep their normal routine, the quicker they heal.

Before the patient went home, I asked if the neighbors or family visit often. That way I know how much support they have. I ask how often they go to the doctors, get their hair done, or go out to eat. I know more about their social life. I ask if they take their own medicine or if someone sets it up for them. I ask if they pay their own bills. How often do they talk on the phone? Do they go to church and how often do they go? I learn to be an advocate in all areas of their life, and usually they come to respect the fact that I care completely about their life not just what I am doing for them physically. I would watch their body language to see if they were uncomfortable talking about things and adjust my questions to this. I have also had my patients write in a journal to understand their routine better, and sometimes they would share their inner thoughts about their fears or anxiety. **I learned to be a friendly advocate.**

I would incorporate hobbies at times to help in the healing process. Sometimes watching body language can tell you when something is happening out of the ordinary. **Be in the moment with them.** Catch any subtle change and be on top of it, it could be the difference between a life threatening problem, or an indication of something more to come. **Always maintain the same tone of voice. I learned that patients can always tell if you are impatient or not present with them.**

**ALWAYS BE PRAYERFUL AND CONFIDENT**

The first rehabilitation center I was in, we had a lot of diverse patients. Orthopedics, amputees, head injuries, strokes, Parkinson's disease, cancer patients, and dementia including Alzheimer. We worked with drug addicts, tuberculosis patients, and diabetics. People were from the poor class to the upper class of society. When I worked with these people, I focused on them one on one and stayed totally present to their care. I became their advocate. When needed, I made sure they had the best therapy possible, worked with their emotional needs to heal, encouraged them at all times and problem solved with them. The most important care I gave them was prayer, sometimes with them, sometimes silently. To this day, I pray for my patients from past care, current patients, and the patients I have not met yet. **Always give your best when caring for others. Treat them like you want to be treated.**

I remember my first patient. He was 6'3, weighed about 250lbs., a bilateral knee replacement that needed assistance transferring to a chair from the bed. I am 5'4 and about 145lbs. I was told to walk in there with the confidence of Hercules and tell him we are transferring to the chair. **I learned a lesson that day. If you exude great confidence in the task at hand, everyone steps up to the plate with that same confidence, even if they don't think they have it.**

He looked at me and said, "Are you sure you can do this," I stated I do it all the time and it will be just fine. (Then I said a little prayer for help and was confident we could do it.) Both knees just replaced, not feeling at ease with the task, my patient initiated more strength than he thought he had and it was relatively easy and safe. After that he stated he did not feel he had the strength but since I was so sure of myself he knew we could do it. **Learn to inspire others to do their best even when they think they are not able to do it. Push them to be their best.**

From that day forward I walked into all my patient's rooms with that confidence. Goals are achieved and people discover they have more strength than they think when it is needed. **Be their confidence until they get theirs back.**

Another patient I remember fondly, I will call Bobby. Bobby had a massive stroke and was sent to us from a big rehabilitation center and told that was the best he would be. Bobby lost his voice, could not help himself with bed mobility, could not walk, and was very frustrated that he could not express himself. His wife was very protective of him and mad at the medical field, because he was not advancing as well as she wanted. Due to the previous place, she demanded to be in therapy every time he was seen and documented every move we made to insure his quality of care. **Bobby taught me the great gift which I thought I had, but enhanced it more, the gift of patience.**

I first learned in order to get the results I needed from Bobby, I needed to allow his wife to express her frustration and anger for the changes that happened to their family. I had to let her know I cared for her as much as I did for Bobby. She soon became calm and trusted my work with Bobby enough to leave the center for periods of time. I learned to communicate with Bobby by learning his body language, watching his gestures, his grunts and what his eyes were telling me. Soon we became a team.

We also had a lot of humor when we were first trying to communicate and would get way off of what he needed. He would shake his head and laugh at us. **Bobby taught me there is humor to be found in any situation if you allow it to happen.** I think we surprised each other and soon became a good team getting good results. Bobby ended up walking out of the center using a straight cane, learning to communicate without a voice, and going home to a quality of life only his wife could give him. They were a great example of the vows people take when they marry. I learned early on to be Bobby's voice, since I worked so closely with him. When someone in the center could not understand his needs, they would call me. **Again, learn to be someone's voice when they cannot be their own voice.** It took me back to my brother's childhood.

One important thing I learned early on in my vocation was the **power of prayer**. I prayed when I was in college that God would place me in the vocation that would service my purpose in life. He blessed me more than I could ever have imagined. I continued to pray for my patients before I met them, while working with them, and after they moved on with their life. At the first place I worked at my friend and fellow therapist, Thevlyn, and I started a prayer group for workers. We started in the dining room at 7:30 a.m. before the day started. Soon we had patients come down and join us for prayer. We were asked to move to a private room, to which we did. The prayer group stayed until Thevlyn and I moved to other positions elsewhere. This alone gave strength to the relationship with patients, knowing we were also praying for them to heal. The process of caring for others and praying for others stepped up the healing process. We are called into a sacred contract to care and pray and help heal each other the best way we know how- through the strength of God and our learned skills, and a lot of faith.

I remember Dema, a dear patient who became a good friend. She was in isolation for a contagious infection. Although it may have been costly for the center, I made a point of suiting up in protective garb and seeing Dema as often as I could. I was told once by a World War II patient when he was in isolation, that being there was worse than anything he had experienced in war. I did not forget those words. Dema and I would pray together, I was also her therapist and we would strengthen both the body and soul while she was healing from this infection. I also learned that due to fear of catching something, a lot of people, even the medical field, are afraid of working with certain people. If I was outside with another patient, I would go by Dema's window and we would wave. I can only imagine what isolation would be like, so I tried to do what I would have liked someone else to do if I was there. One day I was called down to Dema's room right after I came into work. At that time I was told Dema's daughter had died of breast cancer. I said a prayer before I went in to have God give me the strength to do whatever Dema needed. I went into the room. Dema and I held each other while she cried and then she asked me to pray that she has the strength to endure and understand this. We did, and I believe she felt more at peace. I remembered how honored I was to be able to sit and pray with a friend who had lost such a dear person in their life. **I learned a lesson, to be there for a friend even if you are not sure what to do.**

Although prayer is my daily beginning and I call forth all my resources available to me, some miracles stand out more than others. I had a patient I will call Ralph, who was another stroke patient of mine. A kind and gentle man, whose wife was very petite, Ralph was in grave condition when he came to us and his wife said the only way he could go home was if he could walk again.

Ralph was on oxygen, had a peg tube, could not move without help in bed, and was not aware of his surroundings. I learned in the early stages of stroke you become part of their body, to reeducate and repetitively move the body to regain use and knowledge of the body, mind and soul. After a while Ralph would be able to sit up on the edge of bed. I knew his body was working but not his mind. I would verbally tell him step by step of everything we would be doing. I eventually put Ralph in a walking box (that is not the medical term) which kept his body upright so I could place the feet in walking position and do the walking motion for him. I remember wanting him to walk so badly and his muscles just not wanting to respond. One day I was using electrical stimulation to reeducate the muscles and I felt a need to pray over his body while this was going on, so I did. I did this every day after that when I was doing this procedure. About four days later Ralph's hamstrings and quads started responding. Eleven months later, Ralph walked out of the center with a quad cane. The day he left, he told me the first three months he was there, he could not remember. He stated people told him what he did and said, yet he could not recall any of it. I remember Ralph saying to me early on, all he wanted to do was go home. He did not want to be here the rest of his life. My daily prayer included Ralph's daily prayer. **Every day you can give someone the best quality of life for them that**

**day, and that is a small miracle in itself.** I remember fondly taking care of a lot of patients in that facility and thanking God for using me as a vessel during the healing process.

I also learned that all wishes cannot be honored, because it is too painful for the living to carry out those wishes. I had a patient with a brain tumor and all she wanted to do was go home and die in her home. Her husband could not stand the fact that she would die in their home. She died at our center and I was blessed to visit with her daily until she passed. Years later, I have been doing home health and I ended up with her husband as a patient. He looked familiar but, I could not place where I met him until he told me how sorry he was that he did not honor his wife's desire to die at home. He was riddled with guilt. I told him he made the best decision because it was too painful for him and he had great memories to help him through the years in that home. His wife's picture was everywhere and I believed her spirit was there comforting him. **I learned another lesson that day. Each of us dealt with dying in our own way and we need to respect and honor that, not judge it.**

I always felt I was a calm and patient person although I have had my moments. I realized this is a gift. I have seen situations that could have been very stressful for the patient and needed to keep a calm atmosphere so my patients would not panic and increase their fear.

I have seen family members of patients become anxious and feel helpless until they see me calm. We talk through the situation and educate them until they feel a sense of peace with whatever it is they are dealing with.

**Learn to bring peace to whatever situation you are in and things will fall into place with a great sense of calmness.** As I have grown older, hopefully I have grown a little wiser, and have a greater depth for compassion and empathy for each life I encounter. I not only was able to be with patients at their lowest points in life, after befriending them I was able to see them in better health and watch how they went on living and loving. A few close friends come to mind.

One is Louise, she is 99 years old, and is the last of her relatives living in her generation. She feels isolated at times and lost without someone to talk to her that can relate to her past memories. I treated her sister and her brother before they passed, so we have some things to share. Louise teaches me how to endure life with whatever it has to offer. Although pessimistic at times, she ends up laughing about things in general. She has taught me, as well as other elderly patients have, that the medical field is prejudice against the aging.

After a certain age, usually about late 80's early 90's; a lot of the medical field use the language, "What do you expect at this age." Louise went to the doctor for her annual physical when she was 98 and she always gets a card for her next visit. Well, I asked how her doctor's appointment went and she was upset that they did not give her a card for next year's appointment. Her statement was, "I guess they think I won't be here next year so I might as well prepare to die." Other patients have told me that doctors stop talking to them and talk to their children as if they were not in the room. Until someone is proved incompetent, treat them with all the respect you would like to be treated with, and even more when they cannot speak or think for themselves. **I learned to honor and respect every age.**

Another friend, Patty, has become a dear friend over the years. We have more in common. I told her she must have been my sister in another life. She has been through a lot of therapy due to many ailments but she is tough and comes back every time. I have seen Patty go from walking with a walker to being independently wheelchair bound, and living alone. Her spirit changed to the situation. When she lost her husband, Tom, family and friends expressed concern that she may not be capable of living alone. She depended on Tom to do everything for her. She stepped up to the plate, and has been living with herself for a year and a half until her recent ailment. She has taught me that we are stronger than we think. She laughs at how surprised she has been with herself and her own inner strength. **Another lesson I have learned is that people assume when one is in a wheelchair, or appears fragile, then they have something mentally wrong and are not able to be alone. Never judge a book by its cover!**

Educate society with the conditions your family members have and treat them with the honor and respect they deserve. **Let them do whatever they can do for themselves. Let them feel there is a purpose for them to be here, not just sit around and wait for dying to happen.**

My brother, Danny, and sister, Millie, both experienced cancer about a year or so apart from each other. Both demanded that people let them do as much as they were able to do by their self. I believed they healed quicker.

My brother Dale was diagnosed with ALS, also known as Lou Gehrig's Disease. We were all shocked. He drove himself to the doctor July 28, 2010. I went home in September to stay with him for a month. By then, he needed someone there for safety purposes and to transport him to therapy. He wanted to do as much as he could. He explained to me his routine and I watched him for a month and documented his every move of what he was capable of doing.

Dale has a great wife, Patty. She is a woman of great faith. I told her she needed to care for herself so she could care for Dale. Sometimes that means sacrificing times so both of you have the quality of life through this process. I thank God every day that both sides of the family are large and in retirement age. Dale requires around the clock care, and it is all given by family members who know Dale, know his routine, and spend quality time with him meeting his and Patty's needs. Some help with the physical care, some clean the house, some provide the meals, some just come and hang with Dale. Dale has a good friend Bob that came and visited with him and even gave him a massage now and then. I received a card from Dale and Patty early on in this disease process to thank me for setting the atmosphere of peace and calmness as they deal with this journey. Sometimes you don't know the gift you bring until later.

**Although you educate families on the illness's they develop, it is never easy when it is your own, only God's grace helps you through it all. Learn to be present mentally and physically to bring the trust forth from the one you are caring for.** Dale's trust in other people had always amazed me and now more than ever. He had always taken life in stride and enjoyed it as much as he could. We laughed at the stupid stuff that occurs in our ignorance of miscommunication. We cried when he was frustrated, and we thanked God that we could care for him just because we could. Life is to be cherished no matter what condition. Dale was slowly losing his voice as I wrote my book. One day, as it was when I was a child, we will become his voice again. **Master what you do so when the time comes, and you are called to do something, it will flow as easily as water flows down a stream. The greatest of these is Love.**

# IN TIMES OF CHANGE

After nine years in rehabilitation centers, hospital contract work and outpatient, I was beginning to feel defeated by the system and insurance companies on patient care. It became more of a production line than caring for the individual person. I received a phone call the week I was to leave work to look at another type of physical therapy. I was asked if I would be interested in home health. This was one area I had not tried so I said I would give it a whirl. This brought me back to why God placed me in this field: one-on-one care, more quality care with the patient, to look at their real world, and learn how they function.

Teach family members to give the best quality of life possible to the patient in whatever situation they are in. I was also able to befriend patients and their families. We problem solved issues together, improved patient's physical status, kept patients safe, and helped them to reclaim the life they had before their illness or accident. Sometimes I would listen to the patient while we were doing physical therapy. They talked about their fears, their dreams, and their life after death, etc. I learned to minister to their spirit, help heal them physically and emotionally.

Physically healing someone is only part of the issue. What did they lose in the process and can they get it back? How can the family support them better if necessary? Teach them to laugh more at life and themselves. Teach families that patients want to laugh and find humor because they are still living and want to be involved in everyday life.

My brother Dale is unable to do anything physically at this point but he wants to know how everyone is, what is going on, and kept track of the sports he loves. He always looks at life in a humorous way. He is slowly losing his voice and I see he is a little more serious at times, especially when people could not understand what he is trying to say. I could not understand him at times the last time I visited him. When I did not understand him, I told him to excuse his ignorant sister for not knowing what he said, he would roll his eyes with a twinkle. Life throws a curve ball at you and hits you smack in the middle of the face and stuns you temporarily. You stay prayerful, love the best you can, and ask for all the guidance to help each of us through situations we never thought we could endure. **I learned another lesson, joy and sorrow walk side by side in life. It is the ebb and flow of life.** Just do it because you can. Some people would love to but can't. Place yourself in their shoes.

I presently work, as needed, for a home health company and try to improve my skills with every patient, and look for the lesson they have to teach me. Everyone has a lesson to learn and teach. I am in the presence of great wisdom every time I walk into a house. I have learned that each person I come in contact with, either has a lesson to teach me or I have one to teach them. We grow from each other. Everybody reacts different to therapy and to people. I have learned to look at the soul of the person when I encounter them because we are all on this walk together. **Learn to be fully in the present when you are with people and let things go when you go home.** I use to take a lot of people's problems home with me and it would be miserable for me and my family.

I don't own these problems and I cannot solve a lot of them, but I can place them in God's hands and pray for them. **I have**

**learned to give all my worries to God and embrace all life has to offer.** It may appear I am distancing myself from the situation but in fact I am giving it more attention by giving it to God. We are a vessel passing on good care: a vessel of prayer knowing God finishes the picture: a vessel of love; teaching, sharing, non-judging of others at all times. After you step out of the door, leave it to God!

# USE INTEREST OR HOBBIES TO HEAL

One of the greatest healers is nature, or someone's interest in a hobby. It could be reading, writing, gardening, sewing, cooking, woodworking, singing, playing an instrument, etc. Most people enjoy animals and outdoors. If they have a favorite pet, make sure they are able to spend time with them. Animals are very sensitive to people and sense things we don't. If they enjoy the outdoors, get them out as much as possible, even if you have to encourage them. Know what gives them peace, and place them there in the healing process. Include them in the everyday living process of housekeeping, gardening or whatever keeps them active, so they feel worthwhile and not a burden to people.

If depression sets in, get help so it doesn't affect their healing time. When I worked in the rehab centers, we would have dog therapy, bird sanctuary, fish tanks, and they would prove to lower blood pressures and bring patients peace. With men that would work outside a lot, I would have them tend to the bird feeders and do a little weeding if needed. Try to keep things as normal as possible. When my friend Patty became widowed, she occupied herself with her home. She was wheelchair bound but she was able to cook for herself, mop and clean her house. She was not able to get to the washer and dryer so we would wash her clothes and after they were dried, we would bring them in for her to fold. Patty wanted to be able to take care of herself and her home as long as she could. I believe that if she was relieved of those responsibilities, she would have gone into a depression and became sick.

**I learned you give people responsibility for their own welfare, and you give them purpose as long as they can do it.** I have seen children that have let their parents take care of themselves even though they were nervous about it. Everyone had a better quality of life from it. Don't take away one's purpose in life or you will see a decline of health quickly. Another patient of mine, Jane, had a daughter that had her mother tear out seams from clothing for as long as she wanted. Jane found this task interesting due to her years of sewing, and she also found this enjoyable. Simple tasks can be very purposeful to one. Setting and clearing the table, taking out garbage, getting the mail, folding the clothes, changing light bulbs, be as creative and as challenging as you want, but make sure everyone feels they are contributing to the world in which they live.

One very important interest people have is going to church. When one feels a burden to others because they are using an assistive device or wheelchair, they tend to discourage people from taking them to church. This is very life giving to people. Do this transition as soon as possible so people do not feel like they are a burden. Encourage this ritual as much as possible, especially if it has been a big part of their life. We are called to assist just because we can. People who have been active in church most of their lives find this life giving and healing. Make it happen.

**BE IN THEIR WORLD**

I am talking about the world that Alzheimer people live in. I have been blessed to have the opportunity to work in rehab units that have Alzheimer patients. They have taught me much about the world they live in, and not one is the same. I have connected with them at the place they are now, and learned who they were before the disease dominated their life. I have seen the devastation it brings to families. I would see family members in denial, families grieving for their loved one to recognize them, some turn from them due to their change in personality. I have over the years become many people to my Alzheimer patients. I have been their students, their saloon customers, their sister or relative in one manner or another. I have learned to be who they see me as and earn their trust to care for them. It is not always easy.

I remember a patient, Alice, who came to our center with a broken hip. The accident kicked in her Alzheimer's disease more. Alice fought everybody and was very frustrated. I was assigned to Alice for therapy with a broken hip. Guess what? Alice did not want me. **I learned to be consistent and continue to always speak in a gentle and even tone.** I came in everyday to start by telling Alice what the routine would be for the day. Alice hit me, called me many names and tried to get out of doing anything. I stayed persistent in a gentle manner and continued with what was required to get Alice better. Her son did not feel we were giving her the needed therapy, and requested to be in therapy during her scheduled time. Her son came twice. The first time when Alice and I started to walk using her walker, and letting her know what was going to happen, Alice proceeded to hit me and call me all kinds of names. Her son was flabbergasted and told her mom to stop doing that and asked why she was using profanity when he never heard her use it before. We explained before what would happen but, he was in denial. After our walk Alice always patted my leg and said thank you. This was the mom he knew not the other one. We then proceeded with the rest of the therapy, sometimes with much encouragement but not always. Alice came to know I would see to her needs. After therapy was over, I would sometimes be called to the unit because Alice would not let them take her to the bathroom. I would go in and say its time Alice for you and I to do our business. Alice was compliant with me most of the time. She thought I was her sister, so I became who she thought, and we could get what we needed done in a non-defiant manner. To give love is one thing, but to know you will never get it in return is giving of yourself with no expectations of getting anything back. **I learned even if people don't know you, they sure know when they are being loved. Always treat people with dignity.**

When patients or people are doing things and are not aware of it, I remembered Jesus when he prayed and stated "Forgive them Father for they do not know what they are doing." (Luke 23:34) At that time all is well with me and the souls I care for.

# TIME ALONE

Everyone needs time alone for solitude, for reflection, time to pray, and time to just be. In my experiences with working with people in many situations, I have found them to follow a routine. Watch closely and you will notice a time in the day they are content being by themselves, no one hovering over them, conversing with them or trying to fill in their time. This is their sacred space and you need to honor it. Allow it to happen so they can spend some time with themselves to heal, accept what is, and pray for whatever it is they need.

I have two dear friends in their nineties, Patty and Louise. Both are widows now. I've known Louise always as a widow. She likes her time alone. She drove until 2 years ago (she is 99 years old) Louise has always been independent and alone for more than 20 years. She now has to have someone live with her and she finds that very hard. She demands her alone time and her caregiver will go on errands when she becomes a little agitated. Patty recently turned ninety-five (95) and has always had the time of 1:00 pm to 3:00 pm for herself. No one calls or bothers her, this is her nap time.

My brother, Dale, retired two years before he was diagnosed with ALS. He was home alone most of the time. He did the yard work, the housework, and enjoyed his time alone. When I came to stay with him for a month I could tell he required his time by himself as I do. He was not happy someone may be required to stay with him. I watched his routine and found out when he liked his time alone. I would take the dog for a walk, or go off to read alone, I would work, and clean the house the way he liked it clean. I did this the way he expressed he liked it, the way he would have done it. I would start dinner in the kitchen when he would read the paper, or watched sports.  He soon relaxed and realized I was not going to hover over him every moment.  **I learned to honor people's time alone.**

# SPECIAL TREATMENT

People with addictions need special treatment. Even though I was physically taking care of a patient who had drug, alcohol, smoking or other addictions; I needed to address those issues while helping the patient to heal. I remember taking care of an alcoholic who developed dementia along with balance disorders. He required, and had a written prescription for alcohol to prevent Delirium Tremens (DTs) from worsening. Each afternoon he would go up to the nurses desk and holler "set me up". He would receive his little shot of whiskey and go about his way. His body took a lot longer to heal due to his alcoholism but it would have been worse if it wasn't addressed.

I also had a homeless man that fell and broke his hip. He was non-compliant with everyone because he could not have a cigarette. His name was Paul. I always told my family I would not buy them cigarettes or alcohol. The only way I could get Paul to work with me was to tell him if he worked with me I would buy him a pack of cigarettes and take him out for a smoke after therapy, because you could not smoke in the facility. Paul worked as hard as he could if not harder than most in therapy. I kept my end of the bargain and took him for his smoke. The day Paul left the facility I was not there, but he made sure I knew that he wanted to thank me and tell me that not everyone would do what I did. They would, he just didn't know it.

Care for the whole person even if it challenges you. When I went back home for the first time to take care of my brother, I also bought him cigarettes. He was also an alcoholic, and I too bought him beer. It was not my position to change his lifestyle. His lifestyle was changed way too soon for all of us. I even learned to light his cigarette and put a straw in his beer to make it easier for him. You will be challenged, but love overcomes a lot.

# EXPECT TO BE BLESSED

One of the greatest lessons I learned while taking care of patients was during the time my daughter was about to become a mother. My daughter, Carissa, was 19 years old and unwed. I heard and felt some controversy around me with family members, friends, and society as a whole. I expected more criticism from the elderly group I worked with. My dear friend Patty, who I had just met and saw as a patient, gave me a bluebird of happiness. She told me to be happy and enjoy being a grandparent. The patients at that center embraced me and my daughter. Many co-workers came to me with their stories and blessings for the new baby. I was overwhelmed and humbled. The rest of the people came around after the initial news settled in. **Thank God for unexpected blessings! This also allowed me to remember my grandmother's journey being a single parent, and the lessons learned from that period of time.**

Also during this period, the pastor of our church and dear friend, Mark, asked that I write a letter letting everyone know where I stood with my daughter and that there would be no misunderstanding of how we, Mike and I, felt. He also stated to ask for their prayers and support. If they could not give it, then bless them and thank them anyway. I have passed this onto many patients in respect to how they want to be treated, and how people need to support, or remove themselves from the situation.

Another blessing I can recall was from a patient, Jane. Jane was very petite, in her late 80's who came to live with her daughter, Susan. She needed therapy at the time, and I went. Jane's fragile body looked like she could barely help herself. I do not look at this until someone demonstrates they cannot help themselves. Jane was stronger than she gave herself credit for. As we progressed with strength and safety, I asked her if she ever jumped on a trampoline. She looked at me and laughed. Well, Susan happened to have one at her house and after much encouragement, and knowing that the trampoline was a small rebound, she trusted the fact that I would support her and tried it. This was great for increasing balance stability. She had a ball, laughed and giggled like a little girl.

**If possible, help someone experience something they have never done in their life.** Susan and I became friends. I started going to her book club after I stopped seeing her mom for therapy. I was able to continue to see Jane as a friend, share laughter with her, and see her at the end of her journey and support her daughter as much as I could. **The unexpected blessing for me was I met a good friend who is on this wonderful journey of life with me and we can share memories of Jane.**

**DON'T TRY TO BE EVERYTHING**

You have a task at hand. Care for someone the best you can. This can be many things. You could possibly be the driver for doctor appointments, have lunch as a friend, may be a therapist to help heal one, someone who helps with baths, cleaning house, sitting with them, or sharing special times with them. It could be cooking for them or doing their hair. You cannot be all of these all the time. Know your limits, or you will burn out. Ask for help and don't feel it is bothering someone because we are called to help each other when needed. Do the best you can and get many people to do many things so the burden is not so hard. It is a gift to serve others, sometimes they do not know what to do unless you ask.

My sister-in-law, Patty asked family and friends if they could help with the care of my brother and her. The calendar is full each month without asking. She has people who stay with Dale while she works. She has people that have volunteered to cook them meals so she has quality time with Dale. Someone does Dale's lawn at a very reasonable price since he found out Dale is not able too. "Ask and yea shall receive, seek and yea shall find, and knock and the door shall be opened unto you." (Matthew 7:7.) Ask your family, your friends, your church, your community for help. Be prayerful and think outside the box if necessary. Many things are possible.

Dale is a person that has always loved unconditionally and with great joy. People only want to give that back and Patty has allowed this to happen. To give and receive is a great gift.

**BE THERE FOR THE LONELY AND DEPRESSED**

It has always been a heartfelt need, to be with those who experience loneliness or depression. I try to place myself in their shoes and see what it is I would need if I were in that position. I have had many opportunities to help with the increase of single parents, the elderly whom I work with, friends and their children's illness, my own family's struggle with depression and close friend's deaths.

I have talked on the phone until wee hours of the morning to friends who did not know how they were going to get through the night, or how they will raise their children alone.

I have been with friends' children who were very sick to give parents some relief, or even take a spouse out of state to be buried while I watched her child in CCU from a car accident. I have gone away for weekends with girl-friends who have needed a break from their routine or they felt like they were going to lose it. I have had many single people spend time at our home just so they did not have to be alone.

Depression is an illness that some people don't even know they have until a friend expresses concern and care. Being lonely is more common than people realize. This can lead to serious health problems if not aware.

It is not easy to be there for someone and it takes a lot of prayer and gut instinct to know what to do. Sometimes you need to do nothing but sit in their presence and be prayerful. I lost a friend suddenly about 8 years ago and asked my dear friend if she wanted me to spend some time with her. (The dear friend was her husband) I lived in Tennessee and they lived in Michigan.

She said yes, so I opened up some time and flew back to see her. We all need people in our lives that can drop what they are doing and come when needed. I hope that someone will be there for me if the time comes when I will need help.

I took in my girlfriend's children while she finished her last semester of nursing because she was at a breaking point and could not go on unless someone helped.

I befriended a girlfriend's son dying of leukemia until he took his last breath. **I learned children are a lot stronger than we give them credit for.** I took our minister to classes with me because he had eye surgery and could not see and we took turns caring for him. **I learned what it is like teaching a blind person about the geology of unleveled surfaces and getting in and out of building with description only.**

I stayed with my neighbor, whom I just met, in the emergency room when he fell and broke his hip at his home until his family arrived. I would not want to be in emergency alone without someone to support me. He died one week later from complications. The family expressed gratitude, but it was I who was grateful that I could help. Do this just because you can.

It is hard enough to be in a critical situation or have to depend on people when you are alone. Be aware of those around you who are single or lonely, and tend to them like you would have liked to be tended to if it was you. **"Do unto others as would have them do unto you." (Matthew 7:12)**

**RESPONSIBILITY**

A note to remember: Medicine is still an art based on science, so a person in this field is "practicing medicine." Miracles happen, people are cured, some are still trial and error, protocols help but are not always accurate because each body is unique and reacts differently to treatment. Things need to be tweaked to the person's response. We all, the health professionals, patients and their families are responsible in the care of healing and caring for someone. **I learned it is not one person's responsibility to care it is the responsibility of everyone.**

Patients and people will tell you what works and what doesn't. If conventional medicine works, great; but if alternative medicine works, go for it. If you have your own protocol that has worked, share it. I have heard many stories from my arthritic patients on what works for them and a lot of it is not conventional. No one person has the answer. Listen clearly, feel that gut instinct, educate yourself, don't always put your life into a handful of strangers that seem to have the answers, problem solve with them.

Always seek the best care, ask questions, know your rights, and have a trusted advocate with you at appointments to hear what you don't. If someone questions you, don't take it personally, they just want to know what they are doing is right.

It is now March of 2011, and after going home to see my brother recently, I knew I was not needed other than to visit and love Dale and relieve people if needed. I am not so arrogant to think I am the only one who knows how to care for him. Each person with Dale brings his own flavor of how to care for him. All are compassionate and made sure his needs are met. He is loved, and we shared quality time together. Dale is very aware if he did not have his family he would be in the hands of strangers, healthcare people that can take care of his physical needs but not necessarily his emotional needs. He is a man of grace and much gratitude. He gets frustrated with us at times when we cannot understand him but he just shakes it off. He enjoys who he is with and the day that he has been given. That in itself is a miracle.

# CONTINUAL CARE

**I learned after you care for someone try not to end it suddenly if possible.** Send them a note or card to let them know what a privilege is was to care for them. Let them know you will continue to have them in your prayers. Sometimes I just keep in touch at Christmas, sometimes I show up a few months later with some jam or bread just to see how they are doing. I cannot do this with everyone but my gut instinct tells me which ones need a little more tender loving care.

I once had brought dinner to a patient of mine whose daughter went on a cruise and people from her daughter's church were taking care of her while Beverly was gone. I told her daughter that I would come over and have dinner with her one night while she was gone.

I brought a roast beef dinner over and Miss Lillian and I enjoyed good food and had a fine conversation. Miss Lillian never forgot that and neither did I. Just spending time outside of therapy with someone lets them know they are loved and not alone. **Remember, people will remember how you make them feel. Make them feel worthy.**

**KNOW WHEN YOUR CARING IS FINISHED**

As a physical therapist assistant, we follow written orders for goals to be met and then ask for discharge of the patient when the goals are met. Sometimes this happens quicker than other times. Some patients you have for an extended amount of time. Sometimes home health patients are seen over again after a period of time due to the aging process and difficulty with independence due to strength or other illnesses.

I remember fondly a patient with heart disease and rheumatoid arthritis. She worked harder than any patient I had at that time to stay independent. She became chronically ill and each time she was sick it took longer for her to recuperate. She talked of her losses and was concerned about what her son was going to do without her. We worked hard on keeping her walking with an assistive device. I came back from seeing my brother and we had picked this patient back up for strengthening. I knew she was not capable of therapy at that time and tried to explain to her son she was to sick and stressed the fact that she needed to heal more and require different equipment in home to keep her quality of life the best it can be in whatever situation. He felt I was giving up on his mother, but I knew she could not tolerate therapy in her condition. We discharged her from therapy although nursing stayed in. I prayed for her until the day she passed which was a few months later. **I learned to know when it is time to let someone else take over the care. Be prayerful and move on. I learned sometimes people will place expectations on you that you cannot meet.**

Don't take it personal, they are seeking all the miracles they can get. I would too. Know you did the best you could and place it in God's hands. Keep their quality of life the best you can, at whatever condition one is in. Do the changes needed, keep them comfortable and loved. This is compassion and the best you can do while you can.

# TEACH THE GENERATIONS

The years I've been working I have discovered how important it is in the healing process when different generations are involved.

I believe we have done a great disservice by placing the care of our loved ones into other people's hands much too soon. This cannot be a lost gift. Never underestimate the care, the maturity and knowledge of younger generations in the care giving of loved ones. Encouraging and teaching each other to love and care in whatever situations gives value to all of life. It should be as natural as taking care of yourself.

I remember a great grandchild of a patient of mine who cared for her grandmother. The family was poor and most of them had to work and this left the younger ones to care for their mother/grandmother at times. Miss Holly was a great caregiver. She could flush out her grandmother's peg tube, change her bed with her in it (she had a stroke) and she could monitor her oxygen and make sure her oxygen hose was not clogged. She was a good as any nurse and she was young.

My niece Hannah, who is Dale's granddaughter, is very good with her papa. She is nine years old and is as compassionate of a caregiver as there are. She is so tender and loving with her papa. If he needs something, she is right there to help, if he needs to be fed, she will feed him his mounds bars (his favorite), she even jokes and laughs with him. Priceless life is. Even little Ryan (his 16 month old grandson) will go up to him and touch his leg and lay his head on his lap. I learned to learn from the children, what better teachers, unstained by the world and only filled with love. We each have gifts to teach each other no matter what age.

Paul, Dale's son, is a great example of stepping up to care for his father. Paul is in his 20's and moved home within a few months of Dale being diagnosed. He was purchasing a home and wanted to save some money. When Dale was diagnoses Paul stayed home. He has been a pillar for Patty and Dale. You can just see in their eyes how much they love each other. Paul probably knows Dale more that anyone what he needs and likes and wants. Learn from each other and pass it down through the generations so we all know how to love and care for each other as God wants us too. I hope through the examples that people have given me that I to will be a more compassionate and loving person toward others.

My niece, Natalie, Dale's daughter knows exactly what foods her father loves. She gets them for him and you can see his eyes light up. She is also tuned into his changes before anyone else is aware of it.

I have seen brothers and sisters take care of each other, I have seen nieces and nephews take care of aunts and uncles, I have seen many generations living together, and giving each other a quality of life that only living together can give.

My daughter and granddaughter live with us at this moment, because my daughter cannot afford to live on her own in this economy. I am not at all dismayed by this, in fact Mike and I have been blessed to be part of their daily life and I hope they are blessed too. They brought life back into a quiet home. We talk and take care of each other more.

Life is meant to be lived with many generations and I am learning every day from it. **I've learned it is important to teach each generation to love, care for, and enjoy each other while we can.** We have much to learn and so little time to do it.

# PRACTICE TOLERANCE

In the first year of my marriage, tolerance was one thing Mike and I had to learn with each other. We learned to compromise our views as independent people, to increase values as a couple. One thing I learned early in working with people is to be tolerant. I have dealt with many personalities and families. There is not one way of doing things. You have to feel the person out to what they are capable of doing, or if they desire to do anything at all. I work with the patient and let them assist with the goals for improving or healing.

When you approach someone you need to care for remember that a lot of their independence has been taken away temporarily in the healing process. The more you can involve them in decision making, the better the outcome. You may, at times, need to encourage and educate them to the reason you need to do what you are doing. This is important, especially for the well-being of the person to get them back to independence at each person's best potential. Bullying is not an option. Neither is making one feel guilty because you do not think they are doing what they are supposed to do. Respect whatever the situation, work with a positive and respectful attitude with those you are trying to heal.

A while back I sat on council for a mission church. We discussed fruits of the spirit, and we talked a lot about tolerance with others. A professor, Ed, who was on council with me stated that if we could learn to tolerate the diversity we all have, and learn to work together, we could problem solve better and learn to make this world a more compassionate place to live with less violence. In every profession we have, we deal with many types of people. We have a choice, to make life easier for all or miserable for many because we see differences instead of commonalities. I choose to see the commonality.

This world of power and greed leave us making choices that are not always good for us or mankind. Work together. We are souls walking together on this journey, and hopefully we want the best quality of life for everyone, including ourselves.

One of my biggest learning lessons in tolerance was when I worked in a healthcare setting that included the extremely obese, greater than 350 pounds but less than 500 pounds. This weight limit was due to the equipment that could help assist with these patients including wheelchairs, Hoyer lifts, special beds, walkers and more. When these patients came to us, we could see from the look in their eyes how they were treated before. Tolerance was the first thing we taught to the other patients who could not understand how they come to be that size. We learned from each other how to teach the world about this addiction, and why it occurred, and how to help treat each one individually.

There were many hurt souls in those bodies. As we worked together to help heal their wounds and build a healthier body, hopefully more people came to understand their issues, and encourage them to become the person they wanted to be. **The lesson I learned is there are a lot of criticism in this world, more than we would like to admit.**

UNLIMITED POTENTIAL

Everyone at some point in their life has received some form of compassion. Therefore, we always have an opportunity to pass this on and bless someone else with compassion. It is easy, it is more unconditional than you realize, and the blessings from caring for others go beyond your expectations.

Through my years of caring for people, I have seen biased opinions dissolved, prayers answered, been loved unconditionally, and received more in return than I could ever have asked for spiritually, and emotionally. I have learned to laugh at myself more, enjoy doing simple things without complaints; housework, gardening, laundry, cooking, reading, driving, and just plain living with more compassion just because I can. I learned to be more patient with myself, listen to my inner voice and gut instincts as my patients have taught me. This thing called care giving has taught me about the sacred journey we are all on together, and how much unlimited potential we all have working as one. **I have learned to find out about as many resources as possible, so I can help people when they need the help I cannot provide.**

The potential of unlimited knowledge goes on and on. We need to strive to know as much about this area as we can. This moment forward can be the greatest potential of who we are meant to be to each other, physically, emotionally, and spiritually. To be compassionate toward one another, is to be able to reach our best potential and beyond. Go make the difference in your life and someone else's.

Someone once said a person may not remember your name or where you came from, but they will always remember how you made them feel. Learn how it is to let someone feel you really care about them. The last visit with my brother, I gave him a massage everyday with my hand vibrator, from the top of his head to his ticklish feet. When I left to come back home, I told him as I always do, that I love him. He told me he loved me too, and thanked me for making him feel better, and said he did not hurt as much. **Little things mean a lot.**

**KNOW YOUR GIFTS/
LIVE THROUGH YOUR HEART**

I've changed over the years going from left brain thinking to right brain thinking. I have always been prayerful and I have known I have guardian angels helping me on this sacred journey, watching over me and the care I give others. I lived a lot of my life thinking if I do something this way then this good will come of it. Soon enough, I learned life is not meant to be lived that way.

There is a lot of mystery to life. **I've learned to put my life in God's hands, and let the Divinity of all Life guide me to my full purpose in this lifetime. I have learned to recognize my gifts in this life.** I know I am a person of patience, a caring person, a disciplined person, organizer, one who enjoys laughter, and learning to laugh more at myself. I like to be with people and I like my solidarity also. It is a gift to know who you are and where you are going.

There is still a lot I probably do not know about myself yet, but as I work toward the desires I strive for in this life, I will know myself better. I know I can encourage and enrich people's lives if they allow me. I have learned to become more compassionate through the care I give to others.

**I have learned empathy over the years trying to place myself in people's situations and how I would want to be treated. I have learned to be more humble and ask for the people to assist me who have other gifts that I do not have to offer that will bring a better outcome.** I have learned to let go of being so hard on myself and laugh more. I have learned to surround myself with life giving people who challenge me to be my best. A gift I have developed through the years is a more simplistic life. My patients have taught me this. I enjoy cleaning, gardening, reading, walking, music, the beach, the mountains, home, and family and friends more just because I can.

I listen carefully most of the time, and that is a true gift in this day and age with all the new communication gadgets they have out. **I learned the most important thing in life is to love and be loved. Hug more, laugh often, and love much!** I have learned to sit longer and play harder. The touch of another human being is the start of healing.

A gift we all have but don't realize the importance of is a smile. It brightens up the day and costs nothing. If you master anything in life, master caring for and loving all mankind. Master the first time you meet someone, that first impression. Master your kindred spirit toward others, your smile, and your touch as if it was the only one that mattered.

I challenge you to do more foot washing of your loved ones and friends and humble yourself before them. Master love and all it means to you. Master unconditional love and master the power of prayer and all its miracles. "Do unto others as you would have them do unto you" (Matthew 7:12) Life is great and God is good all the time. Strive to be your best, and perfect loving in your life with those who travel with you and around you. Learn your lessons and gifts in this life and you will be blessed beyond belief.

# COMMUNAL LIVING

Sometimes the option of living at your own home is no longer an option. Sometimes the choice is to move in with family members, go into assistive living, group home, or even into a long term setting. People become devastated if it is something they do not want.

The difference is how the people who support and love you handle this situation, and how you adjust to it. This world has allowed us to live independently from others without learning how to live communally. I believe that a lot of people live longer, healthier and in peace when they are living in a communal atmosphere that is based on the same beliefs. People feel safe, and know when they become more dependent due to health issues, that someone is there for them to care for them and not leave them. We all need to feel this way. People who live together adjust to changing situations more than people who live alone. Living within a community gives you more connection, more conversation, caring for others, sparking different interests, praying and worshiping together, eating together, (people who live alone tend to eat less because they have no one to eat with, from my experience) building stronger relationships, intergenerational teachings, and are creating a more compassionate society.

I have had a vision for years of living in a communal setting probably due to the large family I grew up in. I saw the advantages, still do to this day. I see a communal society that is responsible for everyone's welfare; physically, emotionally, spiritually and financially. We share chores, share our gifts, take care of each other when we are sick or dying without going somewhere else. We are together in sickness, and health, a form of sacred contract with each other. We will inspire and encourage each other to be our best, love each other unconditionally, and have no expectations that are unreachable. We will use the gifts that God gave us to enrich each other's lives. We will learn from each other, respect each other, and hopefully, we will be an example of a community with all its diversity that can love one another the best we know how while we are here on this sacred ground. **I have learned that quality of life is taught through everyone you come in contact with in your life.**

**FORGIVE ANE MOVE FORWARD**

I have learned in my life, that to move forward with peace in my journey, forgiveness needs and is required to happen. Whether it is something from the past or something recent, in order to care for those around you unconditionally, you must first forgive unconditionally. I have seen many people with anger, jealousy, and resentment that are miserable and have regrets at the end of their life. Don't let this be you. Your health is affected by this as well as your emotional status whether you believe it or not. **I have learned to let go and let God!!!**

**LEARN EMPATHY**

A very important skill to learn is empathy. Have you ever tried to walk in someone's shoes with cancer? Someone with depression, someone ill, someone lonely, someone who has lost a loved one, someone who lost everything due to economics or bad choices? Have you ever been in a domestic violence situation and tried to assist with it or child abuse and volunteered to help the children understand this is not normal? Have you ever been hungry and without food, or without healthcare? Have you ever been with people with addictions and tried to understand it? Learned what you can do to help people with addictions without becoming co-dependent.? Have you ever befriended an elderly person just because you can? Do you have problems that you have not shared with anyone that if you shared could help you improve your life or others through whatever it is you are going through? Have you ever taken care of someone that totally depends on you for everything from wiping their eyes, scratching their nose, moving their hands and feet for them, or helping them dress as well as hygiene skills and even feeding them because they cannot feed themselves? Have you ever tried to interpret what someone is saying as they slowly lose their ability to speak?

Imagine for a moment one of these situations and place yourself in their shoes. What would you want people to do for you? Would you be bitter and angry and not let people help you at all, or worse, want to take actions because you believe you are a burden to everyone? Do you get irritated with people in wheelchairs or using assistive devices in public and feel they should be at home? Have you ever befriended someone who is so large they have to be weighed on a freight scale and have serious health issues? Have you listened to people talk about them? We are called into this world to help and assist with all situations and learn from these events. I have experienced or empathized with every situation listed and more. Life is sacred and the more I see and try to be empathetic, the more blessed I am to be in and see what it might be like to make a difference in another person's life. They do not want pity or sympathy, they want someone to love them for who they are, and know that they can still live a fulfilling life in whatever the description that might be. In the case of addictions, make sure you understand how to help and not become codependent on the situation, a life that might be different from mine yet still life giving.

The most important thing is just love them. Let them know you are there for them. The hardest thing I have seen in my life with working with people happens to be one of the important people in my life, Dale. He is surrounded by so much love, and tolerance, and sacrificial people who only want the best for him and make life enjoyable for him. As I write this, my brother needs everything done for him except the fact that he can still swallow, and he is barely able to speak and be understood. I can no longer talk to him over the phone without some interpretation from someone staying with him. He requires his nose be scratched by someone else, his tears wiped by a loved one, people hug him so he can still feel the warmth of a loved one and he loves to hug. He needs every hygiene issue to be done by a loved one. Can you put yourself in his shoes? He does not want your pity. He wants to go on with everyday life and enjoy the time he has. **Life goes on and it is what it is, so we find the strength and courage to make every moment count.** Nothing less! Children and elderly need to know they count when they are in an unloving situation, they need to see the hope and promises of one human being caring for another. Just do it. It will change this world quickly.

Do you have empathy toward the people who require assistive devices or wheelchairs in public? I have seen people short with disabled people because it caused them to step back and wait whether they want to or not. We need to teach each other to accept what is and make it a value to bring the best solutions possible for whatever we need to solve to make this world a loving and selfless place to live. Just do it because you can, someday it may be you on the other side. How will you want to be treated? How compassionate have you been to know the sacrifice of others caring for you? Do you feel worthy of others caring for you? Well, you are as worthy as any other person on this earth and this journey you travel is sacred whether you think so or not. Someone will step up to the challenge whether it is a loved one or not. So, imagine yourself in diversity. Try to see how they would feel, or how humbled they are by another human loving them in an unconditional manner, and knowing they are not alone on the journey. You have to be grateful for the opportunity and prayerful for God's guidance with caring for others. You will be blessed.

# VISITING THE SICK

People are very compassionate about showering people with companionship during illness. Be careful even if you are related. I have learned a few things in this process and have known a few things in the process.

Number one, call before you come. It is very frustrating sometimes for the family when one shows up unannounced. People may not want company at that time nor even be prepared to have company.

Number two, keep your time short and sweet. Do not overwhelm the family by staying to long.

Number three, keep your comments simple; they are in your prayers, we are thinking of you, etc. Don't ask why is this happening to good people, how come it happened to them, what's the reason for this or tell similar experiences. They may not want to hear it at that time.

Number four, if you show up to visit, ask if you can help do anything or just do what you see is needed to be done; the dishes, laundry, cook, bring food. If you are asked to stay, then do.

Number five, volunteer to pick up children or do grocery shopping or other errands that are needed to be done.

Number six, make sure before you bring food that the food is needed. Too much food can be overwhelming and goes to waste. Split the time food is brought in.

Number seven, volunteer to sit with the sick to allow the family to take care of other things they need to do. They may decline but at times you would be surprised. Place yourself in their shoes. How do you feel about someone visiting you when you are ill? Would you like to be relieved for a while? How do you feel about food being brought in? If it is something you don't want chances are they don't want it either.

Number eight, when one is really sick do not call continually for an update. Family will call or text when they feel the need. This can be very taxing on people as well as frustrating when they don't need the added stress they already have. Be prayerful and patient with family members who are caring for their loved one.

I have also learned it is nice to stay in touch with families who have loved ones with long term illnesses. It may be a simple card, or a simple phone call. Patients have read me cards from people they had not seen in a long time but wrote to inquire about a loved one. I have seen comfort on a person's face from a phone call knowing someone cares at this time. Text messaging is good if you do not want to let people know how you feel because they cannot hear it in your voice, or do not want to go into a full explanation of what is going on. It gets lonely when a family member's illness is long and people put it out of their minds. People feel isolated and are unable to express their sorrow. It is good to give support and encouragement during these times. Everyone reacts different. Just keep in touch if you can.

BE OPEN MINDED

I have learned that everything I pass on from which I have learned does not always work. Gait belt is one example. This is an assistive device to help lift people up safely without hurting them into a standing position, or transfer from one chair to another.

My brother's caregivers found it easier to lift Dale from his arms since he was stiff and did not move. I have seen people who are able to use different assistive devices than what would have been recommended. I learned to be open minded with different techniques that work with certain people.

Learn to be creative and listen how certain things work for certain people. Some families do not understand why you do what you do until you fully explain it to them. Don't leave anything out because they can only care for their loved ones the better educated they are. The more they know the less fearful they are of the situation. Everyone handles the sickness, the depressed, and the dying different. Each person' style is unique and expressed different. Be empathetic with each person and allow the way they take care of the person to be the best way they know how, and honor that.

A few things about morphine that my sister educated us on when her son was in an automobile accident was that people touching him made him feel like sharp needles were running through his body, the sound of people talking or loud stimulation made the vibrations roar through his body with great agitation and when he was given liquids it felt like it was burning his mouth. Little lessons learned. Remember, this is only one person's experience, yours may be different.

**KEEP THE ENVIRONMENT SAFE AND HEALTHY**

One thing I learned with caring for people is, it is very important to the quality of life, and the safety of someone to become aware of the environment in which they live. It is crucial as we age to look for certain issues that may cause harm to us or increase health problems.

When I first enter someone's home I look to see if anything clutters the pathway in which they walk such as loose objects like rugs. I look for animals that step in their pathway. Animals, especially cats, can cause accidents as we age due to the fact that we are not as flexible to quickly get out of the way when they walk in and around our feet. Cluttered furniture in a house can cause accidents if people are not careful. It is important to have a clear pathway so you do not have to move around objects that could cause you to lose your balance. Worse yet, if you do lose your balance and fall, and you have sharp pointed end tables, or glass end tables, you could really harm yourself. Be aware of this.

Lighting is crucial to someone's safety in a home. A lot of people as they age conserve on energy and leave lights out. Good lighting ensures you can see your pathway and all that is around you. This way you can move throughout your home without any problems. Shadows can make things appear to be in the way of moving if you have poor eyesight. Do not move furniture around if someone has poor vision because they are used to where the furniture is, and it assists with knowing where things are, and keeps one safe as possible.

Weapons and poisons, or pesticides should be kept in a safe place. I could only imagine if someone with poor vision or smell would accidentally ingest a poison or pesticide mistaking it for drinking product. I have seen guns loaded sitting on kitchen tables or in the living room and it makes me nervous to know what accident could come of this in a certain situation. Keep these in a safe place from people or children who may use them accidentally.

The furniture is important to one who is having balance disorders, weakness in general and many neurological problems. Chairs with armrests help keep people to sit safely down with the assist of their arms. The height of the chair is important to help people get up, to low is very difficult for people with weakness disorders, to high of chair may prevent people from having their feet touch the floor. This could cause the lower extremities to swell and numbness to set in, which could cause problem when one goes to stand up and attempt to walk. The bed is important to the safety of people. The height is an issue if one becomes weak. If it is too high it will be difficult to get into, and easy to slip out of when getting out. If it is to low it will be difficult to get out of. Slippery bedspreads can cause someone with difficulty to slide out of bed when getting out, or loose sheets on the edge of bed can cause someone to catch their feet in when getting out of bed and fall.

The bathroom is one of the most important places to make safe. It is very difficult to get on and off the toilet when one becomes weak or disabled. A raised toilet seat with handles to help push up is very important for the independence of a person with disabilities. Safety bars in the bathtub so one can hold onto if needed is important as we age, to prevent falls. A seat in the shower is good for safety from falls. A shower seat bench is excellent, especially the ones that hang outside the bathtub so you can sit down before getting in. There are many assistive devices you can get to help with bathing and dressing, such as long handled sponges, sock aids, assistive devices to reach, etc. Make sure you have a mat in the tub to prevent sliding of feet. Wet floors can cause accidents, so keep the floors dry at all times. There are more handles you can put in the bathroom to assist with balance, see what is needed and do it.

Health issues are very important for the quality of life. Foods can leave people ill when they are not able to smell as well as they use to.

The aging-population often leave food in the refrigerator too long, so help and be aware of what is in the kitchen of someone you care for, and make sure it is not outdated or spoiled.

The kitchen is another area to be especially safe. Make sure the stove is turned off. Make sure if you have rugs that you have gripper material under them so they do not slide. The chairs that are in the kitchen should be easy to pull out and push in so it is not difficult if you are weak or have hand problems. Dishes should be easy to reach so you do not fall if you have balance problems. These are just a few issues to be aware of.

Make sure whoever you see that they are getting enough nutrition and water to keep themselves healthy. Poor nutrition and dehydration is common among the elderly if they are not taking care of themselves properly. Look for signs with people that may not be getting enough to eat, or appear dehydrated, this could become a medical problem very quickly.

Make sure the animals have had their regular shots to prevent passing on anything that could cause harm to the person's health.

Curtains should be kept clean of dust to prevent allergy problems. Check for mold problems that could lead to many health issues. Sufficient heat in the winter and cool air in the summer can keep their health consistent throughout the weather changes.

Make sure you have a fire plan. This is important to everyone so no one is guessing where you are, or if you got out. Discuss it with family the easiest way in and out whatever area of the house you are in, and where you will meet outside.

If someone needs oxygen, make sure you make all people aware of how important it is to keep from tripping over the hose, which could cause you and the person using oxygen harm. Keep the hose as close to the outside path of walking as possible. The person using oxygen becomes aware very quickly how important it is on keeping the hose away from the walking path, follow their lead and imagine yourself using this. That may be more helpful in understanding the safety of keeping the hose loose for air to flow easily and safely away to prevent tripping over it.

This applies to assistive devices too. Keep the pathway clear and wide if possible to prevent the device from catching the edge of something, and tipping over causing the person to fall. Help make the environment as friendly, and safe as possible when using an assistive device for you and the person us it.

Getting in and out of the house safely is an important factor. Rails may need to be put in to safely allow one to go in and out of home. This is even more important if someone lives alone and has disabilities. Steps are a safety issue that needs to be addressed. Uneven steps can be an accident waiting to happen if someone has perception problems, and assumes all the steps are equal. People with hip and knee problem ambulate up and down shorter width steps, 4 to 6 inches better than higher steps. Ramps may be needed to increase safety and independence. Be careful of inclines or curbs around homes that may increase the chances of falls. If possible have the mailbox placed closer to the home for safety. This has to be done with a doctor's order. Make sure the locks on the doors are easy to operate which is an important aspect to people with hand problems or weakness disorders. Make sure one can get out of the house safe and easy if alone.

Your phone system is a lifeline. Make sure it works properly. If someone has visual problems, make sure the numbers are large, or be a voice activated phone. If you can, program numbers into the phone to make it easier for someone to call. Have an emergency call plan so someone does not have to think the situation through if an emergency comes up, a plan is already in effect. If possible, when one lives alone, and has any disability at all have a lifeline put in to keep that person safe. This assures quick response if an accident occurs.

Weather can be a safety issue. Have a plan when the weather gets bad and you have to take cover. If you live alone let someone know where you take cover, so if they come to check on you they know where you will be if you need help.

I am sure there are more things to increase a safe and healthy environment in the home, these are just a few. Keep the ones you care for in the best environment possible, this will allow to continue the best quality of life possible.

**BE GRATEFUL, AT PEACE AND FULL OF JOY**

I have learned that to have gratitude is to be humbled with God's blessings and promises. We take much for granted; our health, our relationships, our vocations, our friends, and everyday living. The more grateful I am, the more I feel part of the whole of the universe and nothing less. We are all connected while we travel this human journey and when we move into the spiritual realm of passing from this form to another. I am grateful to learn all the diversity, the challenges and gifts that life has to offer. God expresses himself in many ways that surpasses all understanding. The greatest gift I am grateful for is to be able to love and be loved.

I did not intend to finish this book with the passing of my brother. I wanted him to read it, and help me add his view to it but it was not meant to be. I had not been able to talk to Dale over the phone since March without interpretation and that was difficult. God is good.

On April 23, 2011 I called Dale to wish him a happy birthday and he talked to all four of my family members including me. He told all of us thank you and asked how the weather was and told each of us he loved us and would see him soon. We planned on going home in June. May 4, Dale took a turn for the worse, and was given 24 hours on May 6. We traveled home to say our goodbyes, and Dale lived until May 10, 2011 when, around 11:28 p.m., he took his last breath. I was able to stay with Dale and his family one more time on May 7 helping administer his medication. He could hear us but could not respond. My brother was described as a bad to the bone, rocking rolling, trail blazer and he was that to his last breath. I was loved and was able to love him.

I thank God for my brother and his family who let us be with him this past year and help with his care. To give is great but Dale taught us the greatest lesson, to receive. Dale never did much alone. He enjoyed people, and found humor in everything (even his disease at times). Dale invited us along for the ride with ALS. He knew (even though we may not have) that this was going to be the journey of his life and he wanted everyone who loved him to come along for the ride, good or bad. We laughed, we cried, we prayed, we learned, we shared, we sang, we danced. We shared meals together and shared many stories we had in our lifetime. Life was always good as far as Dale was concerned. He had a loving family, wife of 31 years, two wonderful children, and two grandchildren who were his whole life. What could be any better than that? Dale walked the talk, he loved, he enjoyed, and he left with the courage of which heroes are made. We have been blessed. Live life to the fullest, embrace your gifts, love others with your whole heart, and always above anything else give thanks to God!

Peace comes from knowing our God and knowing you are never alone. Life is what it is. Birth, living in between, and dying are all part of life. Embrace every aspect. Be at peace with whatever is and look through the eyes of unconditional love and see that all is good. The peace of God surpasses all understanding. As Jesus told his disciples in the book of John--14:27, "Peace I leave with you, my peace I give to you." I do not give to you as the world gives. Do not let your heart be troubled, and do not let them be afraid."

Joy is found in loving and caring for others. Joy walks side by side with sorrow, with crying and laughing, it is a feeling that walks side by side with peace. The joy of knowing all is well with my soul is all that is needed to embrace life to the fullest. I learned in this sacred journey called life that the joy in my heart and the peace I have deep within allows me to care for those who cannot necessarily love themselves and do it just because we can.

At Dale's funeral service, the pastor recalled a story from the Bible, (Mark 2:1-5) about the paralytic who was being carried on a board by four men and was trying to get to Jesus but the crowd was too congested. They went to the roof and opened a space up and lowered him down to Jesus. He talked about the faith of the men in caring for their paralytic friend. He stated that is how Dale was taken care of. What a visual blessing!

Be that friend just because you can. The blessing that comes from loving another person in their journey is beyond understanding it is only felt from the heart. No greater love than to love another human being in all its diversity, its joy, its sorrow, its memorable walk with the sacred. This too shall end, so embrace every moment and be grateful, full of peace, and filled with joy in all you do.

# CONCLUSION

As I conclude this book, I know there are many lessons not mentioned and I also know that there are many more to learn. I embrace the sacred journey I travel on and look forward to each day to learn something new, meet new people and continue to work toward the goals I have to make this world a better place to live, one life at a time.

I challenge you to take one person and devote loving energy to care for them as you would like to be cared for. If you are the one that needs the care, remember, people cannot read your mind, you need to ask for help and don't be afraid. People as a whole want to help. Sometimes they just don't know what to do, and need guidance in this area. It may be out of their comfort zone. It is a lesson to be learned with great love and compassion.

Keitha James is a licensed physical therapist assistant in the state of Tennessee. She has worked in many settings in the field of physical therapy for over seventeen years.

She was born in Michigan and transitioned to Tennessee in 1990 with her family. She is currently living in the small community of Glendale with her husband of thirty-six years, Michael, her daughter, Carissa, and her granddaughter, Ashlind Sky.

Keitha enjoys reading, gardening, walks in the country setting, women groups, especially her bunco group who have been together over eleven years, and celebrating tea time with friends. She also enjoys cooking, time alone, and time spent with her family. She is inspired by the people she meets who are challenged in everyday living. She believes one of the best things for our good health is laughter, love and again, laughter.

Web Site: BecauseYouCan.kjj2011.weebly.com